HANDEL

Israel in Egypt

1738

a sacred oratorio for 2 sopranos, alto, tenor &
2 bass soli, SATB & orchestra

*Edited, & the piano accompaniment
arranged by Mendelssohn*

Order No: NOV 070126

NOVELLO PUBLISHING LIMITED
14/15 Berners Street, London W1T 3LJ

ISRAEL IN EGYPT.

PART THE FIRST.

RECIT.

Now there arose a new king over Egypt, which knew not Joseph ; and he set over Israel taskmasters to afflict them with burthens, and they made them serve with rigour.

Ex. i. 8, 11, 13.

CHORUS.

And the children of Israel sighed by reason of the bondage, and their cry came up unto God. They oppressed them with burthens, and made them serve with rigour ; and their cry came up unto God.—*Ex.* ii. 23.

RECIT.

Then sent He Moses, His servant, and Aaron whom He had chosen ; these shewed His signs among them, and wonders in the land of Ham.

He turned their waters into blood.

Ps. cv. 26, 27, 29.

CHORUS.

They loathed to drink of the river. He turned their waters into blood.

Ex. vii. 18, 19.

AIR.

Their land brought forth frogs, yea, even in their king's chambers.—*Ps.* cv. 30.

He gave their cattle over to the pestilence ; blotches and blains broke forth on man and beast.—*Ex.* xi. 9, 10.

CHORUS.

He spake the word, and there came all manner of flies and lice in all their quarters.

He spake ; and the locusts came without number, and devoured the fruits of the ground.—*Ps.* cv. 31, 34, 35.

CHORUS.

He gave them hailstones for rain ; fire mingled with the hail ran along upon the ground.—*Ps.* cv. 32 ; *Ex.* ix. 23, 24.

CHORUS.

He sent a thick darkness over the land, even darkness which might be felt.—*Ex.* x. 21.

CHORUS.

He smote all the first-born of Egypt, the chief of all their strength.—*Ps.* cv. 36, 37.

CHORUS.

But as for His people, He led them forth like sheep : He brought them out with silver and gold ; there was not one feeble person among their tribes.—*Ps.* lxxviii. 53 ; cv. 37.

CHORUS.

Egypt was glad when they departed, for the fear of them fell upon them.

CHORUS.

He rebuked the Red Sea, and it was dried up.—*Ps.* cvi. 9.

He led them through the deep as through a wilderness.—*Ps.* cvi. 9.

But the waters overwhelmed their enemies, there was not one of them left.—*Ps.* cvi. 11.

CHORUS.

And Israel saw that great work that the Lord did upon the Egyptians ; and the people feared the Lord, and believed the Lord and His servant Moses.—*Ex.* xiv. 31.

PART THE SECOND.

CHORUS.
Moses and the children of Israel sung this song unto the Lord, and spake, saying: I will sing unto the Lord, for He hath triumphed gloriously; the horse and his rider hath He thrown into the sea.—*Ex.* xv. 1.

DUET.
The Lord is my strength and my song; He is become my salvation.—*Ex.* xv. 2.

CHORUS.
He is my God, and I will prepare Him an habitation; my father's God, and I will exalt Him.—*Ex.* xv. 2.

DUET.
The Lord is a man of war: Lord is His name. Pharaoh's chariots and his host hath He cast into the sea; his chosen captains also are drowned in the Red Sea.—*Ex.* xv. 3, 4.

CHORUS.
The depths have covered them: they sank into the bottom as a stone.—*Ex.* xv. 5.

CHORUS.
Thy right hand, O Lord, is become glorious in power; Thy right hand, O Lord, hath dashed in pieces the enemy.—*Ex.* xv. 6.

CHORUS.
And in the greatness of Thine excellency Thou hast overthrown them that rose up against Thee.—*Ex.* xv. 7.

CHORUS.
Thou sentest forth Thy wrath, which consumed them as stubble.—*Ex.* xv. 7.

CHORUS.
And with the blast of Thy nostrils the waters were gathered together, the floods stood upright as an heap, and the depths were congealed in the heart of the sea.—*Ex.* xv. 8.

AIR.
The enemy said, I will pursue, I will overtake, I will divide the spoil; my lust shall be satisfied upon them; I will draw my sword, my hand shall destroy them.—*Ex.* xv. 9.

AIR.
Thou didst blow with the wind, the sea covered them; they sank as lead in the mighty waters.—*Ex.* xv. 10.

CHORUS.
Who is like unto Thee, O Lord, among the gods? Who is like Thee, glorious in holiness, fearful in praises, doing wonders?

Thou stretchedst out Thy right hand, the earth swallowed them.—*Ex.* xv. 11, 12.

DUET.
Thou in Thy mercy hast led forth Thy people which Thou hast redeemed; Thou hast guided them in Thy strength unto Thy holy habitation.—*Ex.* xv. 13.

CHORUS.
The people shall hear, and be afraid: sorrow shall take hold on them: all the inhabitants of Canaan shall melt away: by the greatness of Thy arm they shall be as still as a stone; till Thy people pass over, O Lord, which Thou hast purchased.—*Ex.* xv. 14, 15, 16.

AIR.
Thou shalt bring them in, and plant them in the mountain of Thine inheritance, in the place, O Lord, which Thou hast made for Thee to dwell in, in the Sanctuary, O Lord, which Thy hands have established.—*Ex.* xv. 17.

CHORUS.
The Lord shall reign for ever and ever.—*Ex.* xv. 18.

RECIT.
For the horse of Pharaoh went in with his chariots and with his horsemen into the sea, and the Lord brought again the waters of the sea upon them; but the children of Israel went on dry land in the midst of the sea.—*Ex.* xv. 19.

CHORUS.
The Lord shall reign for ever and ever.—*Ex.* xv. 18.

RECIT.
And Miriam the prophetess, the sister of Aaron, took a timbrel in her hand; and all the women went out after her with timbrels and with dances. And Miriam answered them:—*Ex.* xv. 20, 21.

SOLO AND CHORUS.
Sing ye to the Lord, for He hath triumphed gloriously; the horse and his rider hath He thrown into the sea.—*Ex.* xv. 21, 18.

PART I.

RECIT.—"NOW THERE AROSE."

serve, . . . they oppress'd them with burdens,and made them serve,and made them
serve, they oppress'd them with burdens, and made them serve, and they made them
and . . . . their cry . . . . came up un - to God, . . .
and . . . . their cry . . . . came up un - to God, . . .
serve, they oppress'd them with burdens, and made them serve, and made them serve, and made them
serve, and their cry . . . . came up un - to God, . . their
and . . . . their cry . . . . came up un - to God, . .
and . . . . their cry . . . . came up un - to God, . .
serve . . . with rig - our, and they made them serve ;
serve . . . . with rig - our ;
and they made them
they oppress'd them with burdens,and made them serve . . . with rig - our ; they
serve . . . with rig - our ; and they made them serve ;
cry . . . . . . came up un - to God, . . and they made them
they oppress'd them with burdens ;
they oppress'd them with burdens,and made them serve . . . with rig - our ;

and .. the chil-dren of Is - ra - el sigh'd by rea - son of ... the

sigh'd, sigh'd, sigh'd, sigh'd by rea - son of . . the

chil - dren of Is - ra - el sigh'd, sigh'd by rea - son of the

sigh'd, sigh'd, sigh'd, sigh'd by rea - son of . . the

sigh'd, the chil - dren of Is - ra - el sigh'd by rea - son of . . the

and .. the chil - dren of Is - ra - el sigh'd by rea - son of . . the

and .. the chil - dren of Is - ra - el sigh'd by rea - son of . . the

sigh'd, sigh'd, sigh'd, sigh'd by rea - son of . . the

bond - age, they oppress'd them with burdens, and made them serve, ...

bond - age, they oppress'd them with burdens, and made them

bond - age, they oppress'd them with

bond - age,

bond - age, they sigh'd, sigh'd, sigh'd,

bond-age, they sigh'd, sigh'd, sigh'd,

bond-age, they sigh'd, sigh'd, sigh'd,

serve with rig - - our, and . . . their cry . . .
serve with rig - - our. and . . . their cry . . .
serve with rig - - our, and . . . their cry . . .
serve with rig - - our, and . . . their cry . . .
serve with rig - - our, and . . . their cry . . .
serve with rig - - our, and . . . their cry . . .
serve with rig - - our, and . . . their cry . . .
serve with rig - - our, and . . . their cry . . .
came . . up, . . came . . up . . un - - to God.
came . . up, . . came . . up . . un - - to God.
came . . up, . . came . . up . . un - to God.
came . . up, . . came . . up . . un - - to God.
came . . up, . . came . . up . . un - - to God.
came . . up, . . came . . up . . un - - to God.
came . . up, . . came . . up . . un - - to God.
came . . up, . . came . . up . . un - - to God.

No. 3. RECITATIVE.—"THEN SENT HE MOSES."

Then sent He Moses, His servant, and Aaron, whom He had chosen, these shew'd His signs among them, and wonders in the land of Ham. He turn-ed their waters in-to blood:

No. 4. CHORUS.—"THEY LOATHED TO DRINK."

They loathed to drink of the riv-er, He turn-ed their wa-ters into blood, in-to blood; they

AIR.—"THEIR LAND BROUGHT FORTH FROGS.'

bers.   Their

land brought forth frogs,   frogs,   their land brought forth frogs,   yea,

e - ven in their kings' cham - - - - - - - - - - bers, in their

kings' cham - bers.   He gave their cat-tle

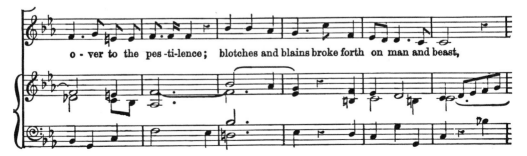

o - ver to the pes -ti-lence;   blotches and blains broke forth on man and beast,

blot- ches   and blains,   blot- ches   and blains broke forth on man and beast, broke

forth, ...   broke forth on man and beast,

blot- ches   and blains,   blot- ches   and blains broke forth .   .   .   .   .

.   .   .   .   on man and beast, broke forth

Adagio.

on man and beast.
a tempo.
Adagio.

Handel's "Israel in Egypt."—Novello, Ewer and Co.'s Octavo Edition.

DOUBLE CHORUS.—"HE GAVE THEM HAILSTONES."

CHORUS.—"HE SENT A THICK DARKNESS."

strength, ... the chief of all . . . . their

the chief of all . . . their strength, the chief . . of all . . their

the chief of all, ... of all their strength, the chief, the chief of all their

the chief of all, ... of all their

strength, He smote all the first-born of E - gypt, the chief, the chief of all their strength.

strength, He smote all the first-born of E - gypt, the chief, the chief of all their strength.

strength, He smote all the first-born of E - gypt, the chief, the chief of all their strength.

strength, He smote all the first-born of E - gypt, the chief, the chief of all their strength.

CHORUS.—"BUT AS FOR HIS PEOPLE."

Handel's "Israel in Egypt."—Novello. Fwer and Co.'s Octavo Edition.

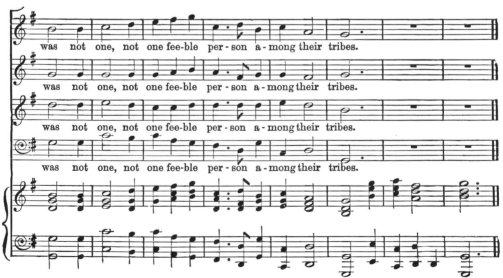

D

Handel's " Israel in Egypt."—Novello, Ewer and Co.'s Octavo Edition.—(49.)

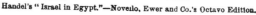

DOUBLE CHORUS.—"HE REBUKED THE RED SEA."

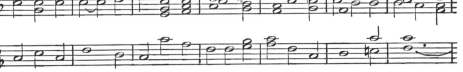

Lord and His serv - - ant Mo - ses; and the peo - ple fear - ed the

- - - - - - ant Mo - ses; and the

serv - - - ant Mo - ses; and the peo - ple fear-ed the Lord, and the

- ses, His serv - ant Mo - ses;

Lord, and the peo - ple fear-ed the Lord, and be - liev- ed the Lord, be- liev- ed the

peo - ple fear - ed, fear - ed the Lord, and be- liev- ed the

peo - ple fear - ed, fear- ed the Lord, and be- liev- ed the

and the peo - ple fear-ed the Lord, and be liev- ed the

Lord and His serv - ant .. Mo - ses.

Lord and His serv - ant Mo - ses.

Lord and His serv - ant .. Mo - ses.

Lord and His serv - ant Mo - ses.

END OF THE FIRST PART.

PART II.

Double Chorus.—"MOSES, AND THE CHILDREN OF ISRAEL."

72

the horse and his rider, the horse and his rider hath He thrown in-to the sea, the

He thrown in - to the sea, the horse and his ri - der, the horse and his ri - der hath
He thrown in - to the sea, the horse and his ri - der, the horse and his ri - der hath
He thrown in - to the sea, the horse and his ri - der, the horse and his ri - der hath
He thrown in - to the sea, the horse and his ri - der, the horse and his ri - der hath
He thrown in - to the sea, the horse and his ri - der, the horse and his ri - der hath
He thrown in - to the sea, the horse and his ri - der, the horse and his ri - der hath
He thrown in - to the sea, the horse and his ri - der, the horse and his ri - der hath
He thrown in - to the sea, the horse and his ri - der, the horse and his ri - der hath
He thrown in- to the sea. I will
He thrown in - to the sea.
He thrown in - to the sea.
He thrown in - to the sea. I will sing . . . . .
He thrown in - to the sea. I will
He thrown in - to the sea.
He thrown in- to the sea.
He thrown in - to the sea. I will sing . . . . .

sing . . . . un - to the Lord, for He
I will sing . . . un - to the Lord, for He hath tri-um-phed
I will sing un - to the Lord,
. . un - to the Lord, for He
sing . . . . un - to the Lord, for He
I will sing . . . un - to the Lord, for He hath tri-um-phed
I will sing un - to the Lord,
. . un - to the Lord, for He
hath triumphed glor - - - - - ious-ly, He hath tri-umphed glor- iously, the
glor - - - iously, glor - iously, gloriously, He hath tri-umphed glor- iously, the
for He hath triumphed glorious - ly, glorious-ly, He hath tri-umphed glor- iously, the
hath triumphed glor - - - - - ious-ly, He hath tri-umphed glor- iously, the
hath triumphed glor - - - - - ious-ly, He hath tri-umphed glor- iously, the
glor - - - iously, glor - iously, glorious-ly, He hath tri-umphed glor- iously, the
for He hath triumphed glor-ious - ly, glorious-ly, He hath tri-umphed glor- iously, the
hath triumphed glor - - - - - - - ious-ly, He hath tri-umphed glor- iously, the

1st
TREBLE.

2nd
TREBLE.

PIANO.

𝅘𝅥 = 112.

The

Lord   is   my strength and my   song,   The

The   Lord   is   my   strength and my song,

He is be-come my sal - va - - - tion, my sal - va-tion, my sal-va -

- va - - tion, my sal - va - - -

- tion, He is become my sal-va - - - - - tion,

- tion, He is become my sal - va -tion, my sal - va - - - tion,

mf

He is become my sal -va - - tion, my salva -

He is become my sal -va - - - - - - tion, my sal-

p

- tion, my sal - va - - tion, He is be-come

- va - - tion, my salva - - - tion, He is be-come

f

my sal-va - - - - - - - - - - - - - - - -

my sal-va - - - - - - - - - - - - - - - -

- - - tion, my sal - va - - tion.

- - - tion, my sal - va - - tion.

Handel's " Israel in Egypt."—Novello, Ewer and Co.'s Octavo Edition.

Handel's "Israel in Egypt."—Novello, Ewer and Co.'s Octavo Edition.

Duet.—"THE LORD IS A MAN OF WAR."

The Lord is a man of war,   The Lord,   the Lord   is

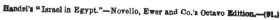

Handel's "Israel in Egypt."—Novello, Ewer and Co.'s Octavo Edition.—(91.)

a man of war,

2nd BASS.

The Lord is a man of

The Lord is a man of war. . . . .

war.

The Lord is a man of war . .

. . . . . . the Lord, the Lord is a man of war.

Lord is His name, . . is His

name, Lord is his name, . . is his name, . . ,

Lord, Lord is his name, . . is . . his name,

Lord is his name, ... is his name,

Lord is his name, . . is his name, . . . Lord is his

Lord is his name, Lord is his name.

name, Lord is his name, Lord . . . is his name.

Pha- raoh's chariots, and his host,

Pha - raoh's chariots, and his host, hath he

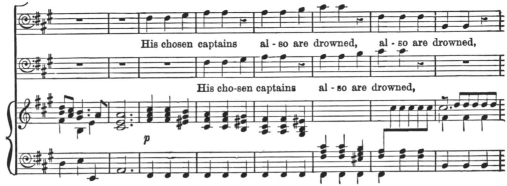

His chosen captains al - so are drowned, al - so are drowned,

His cho-sen captains al - so are drowned,

are drown - - - - - ed, are drown -

al - so are drowned, are drown - - - -

- - ed in the Red sea, his cho-sen captains al - so are drowned,

- - ed in the Red sea, his cho-sen captains al - so are

Handel's "Israel in Egypt."—Novello. Ewer and Co.'s Octavo Edition.

al - so are drowned, al - so are drowned, his cho - sen

drowned, al - so are drowned, his cho - sen

cap-tains al - so are drown-ed, al - so are drown- ed in the Red sea,

cap-tains al - so are drown-ed, al - so are drown- ed in the Red sea,

al - so are drown - - - - ed,

al - so are drown - - - ed, al - so are drown - - - -

- - ed in the Red sea, his cho-sen cap-tains al - so are drowned,

- - ed in the Red sea, his cho-sen cap-tains al - so are drowned,

al - so are drown-ed in the Red sea.

al - so are drown-ed in the Red sea.

Double Chorus.—"THY RIGHT HAND, O LORD."

glor - - ious in pow-er. Thy right hand, O Lord, Thy right hand, O Lord, is
glor - - ious in pow-er, Thy right hand, O Lord, Thy right hand, O Lord, is
glor - - ious in pow-er, Thy right hand, O Lord, Thy right hand, O Lord, is
glor - - ious in pow-er, Thy right hand, O Lord, Thy right hand, O Lord, is
glor - - ious in pow-er, O Lord, Thy right hand, O Lord, is
glor - - ious in pow-er, O Lord, Thy right hand, O Lord, is
glor - - ious in pow-er, O Lord, Thy right hand, O Lord, is
glor - - ious in pow-er, O Lord, Thy right hand, O Lord, is
be - come glor-ious in pow - er,
be - come glor-ious in pow - er,
be - come glor - ious in pow - er, Thy right hand, O Lord, hath dash - ed in
be - come glor - ious in pow - er,
be - come glor - ious in pow - er,
be - come glor - ious in pow - er,
be - come glor - ious in pow - er,
be - come glor - ious in pow - er,

the e - - - - ne - my, Thy right hand, O Lord, hath dash-ed in
piec -es, Thy right hand, O Lord, hath dash-ed in piec - es the e - ne - my,
Thy right hand, O Lord, hath dash- ed in piec - es, in piec - es the e - ne - my,
Thy right hand, O Lord, hath dash-ed in piec - es the e - - - - - - ne -
the e - - - - ne - my, Thy right hand, O Lord, hath dash-ed in
piec - es, Thy right hand, O Lord, hath dash-ed in piec - es, hath dash-ed in piec - es the e - ne -
Thy right hand, O Lord, hath dash-ed in piec - es, hath dash-ed in piec - es the e - ne -
Thy right hand, O Lord, hath dash-ed in piec - es the e - - - - ne -
piec - es, Thy right hand, O Lord, Thy right hand, O Lord, hath dash-ed in
Thy right hand, O Lord, Thy right hand, O Lord, hath dash-ed in
Thy right hand, O Lord, Thy right hand, O Lord, hath dash-ed in
- my, Thy right hand, O Lord,
pie - ces, Thy right hand, O Lord,
- my, Thy right hand, O Lord,
- my, Thy right hand, O Lord,
- my, Thy right hand, O Lord,

piec - es, hath dash - ed in piec-es the e - ne - my.
piec - es, hath dash - ed in piec-es the e - ne - my.
piec - es, hath dash - ed in piec-es the e - ne - my.
Thy right hand, O Lord, hath dash-ed in
Thy right hand, O Lord, hath dash-ed in
Thy right hand, O Lord, hath dash-ed in
Thy right hand, O Lord, hath dash-ed in
Thy right hand, O Lord, hath dash-ed in
Thy right hand, O
Thy right hand, O
Thy right hand, O
piec - es, hath dash - ed in piec-es the e - ne - my, Thy right hand, O
piec - es, hath dash- ed in piec-es the e - ne - my, Thy right hand, O Lord,
piec - es, hath dash- ed in piec-es the e - ne - my, Thy right hand, O Lord,
piec - es, hath dash- ed in piec-es the e - ne - my, Thy right hand, O Lord,
piec - es, hath dash- ed in piec-es the e - ne - my, Thy right hand, O Lord,

Thy right hand, O Lord, Thy right hand, O
Thy right hand, O Lord, Thy right hand, O
Thy right hand, O Lord, Thy right hand, O
Thy right hand, O Lord, Thy right hand, O

piec - es the e - ne - my, Thy right hand, O Lord, Thy right hand. O
piec - es the e - ne - my, Thy right hand, O Lord, Thy right hand. O
piec - es the e - ne - my, Thy right hand, O Lord, Thy right hand, O
piec - es the e - ne - my, Thy right hand, O Lord, Thy right hand, O

Lord, hath dash - ed in piec - es, hath dash- ed in piec - es the e - ne - my.
Lord, hath dash - ed in piec - es, hath dash- ed in piec - es the e - ne - my.
Lord, hath dash - ed in piec - es, hath dash- ed in piec - es the e - ne - my.

Lord, hath dash - ed in piec - es, hath dash- ed in piec - es the e - ne - my.
Lord, hath dash - ed in piec - es, hath dash- ed in piec - es the e - ne - my.
Lord, hath dash - ed in piec - es, hath dash- ed in piec - es the e - ne - my.

Thy wrath, Thou sent
Thou sent - est forth Thy wrath, Thou
Thy wrath, which con - sumed, which con - su - med them, Thou sent -
Thy wrath, which con - sumed, which con - su - med them as stub-ble, Thou
Thy wrath, which con - sumed them as stubble,
Thy wrath, which con - sumed them as stubble,
Thy wrath, which con - su-med, which con-sumed them as stubble,
Thy wrath, which con - su-med, which con-sumed them as stubble,
- est forth Thy wrath, which con - su - med them as
sent - est forth Thy wrath, which con - su-med them as
- est forth Thy wrath, which con- su - med them as
sent - est forth Thy wrath, which con -sumed, which con - su - med them as
which con - su-med them, which con - su - med them as
which con - su-med them, which con - su - med them, which consumed
which con - su-med them, which con -sumed, which con - su - med them as
which con - su-med them, which con - su - med them as

in the heart of the sea.

in the heart of the sea.

in the heart of the sea.

in the heart of the sea.

AIR.—"THE ENEMY SAID."

-vide, ... I'll di -

-vide, I will pur-sue, I will over-take, I will di-

-vide . . . . the spoil :

the e-nemy said, I will pur-sue,

I will o-ver-take, ... I will pur-sue, I'll o-ver-

take, I will di - vide .... the spoil: my lust shall be sa -tis- fied, ... up - on them: I will draw my sword: my hand shall des - troy .... them, I will draw my sword: my hand shall des - troy .... them, my

hand shall des - troy . . . them, I will pur - sue, I'll o - ver -take I will di - vide, I'll draw my sword; my hand shall des - troy . . . . them, my hand, my hand shall des - troy . . them.

Air.—" THOU DIDST BLOW."

Handel's " Israel in Egypt."—Novello, Ewer and Co.'s Octavo Edition.—(129.)

blow, Thou didst blow with the wind; the sea co-ver'd them; they sank, they sank as

lead, they sank as lead in the mighty wa - - - - - - -

- - ters, as lead . . . . in . . the mighty wa - - - - - ters.

Double Chorus.—" WHO IS LIKE UNTO THEE?"

Who is like unto Thee, O Lord, among the Gods? who is like Thee, glorious in

ho - li - ness, fear-ful in prais- es, do-ing wonders, Thou stretchest out Thy right hand.

DOUBLE CHORUS.—"THE EARTH SWALLOWED THEM."

the earth swal - - - - - - low'd them, the . . earth swal - - -
them, the . . earth swal - - - - - - low'd, swal - low'd them, the
- - low'd them, the earth swal- low'd, swal - -
- - - - - low'd them, the . . earth swal -low'd, swal- low'd them,
The earth swal - - - - - - low'd them, the . . earth swallow'd,
The . . earth swal - - - - - - low'd them, the earth
The earth swal- low'd, swal - - -
The . . earth swal- low'd, swal- low'd them,
- - low'd them, swal - - - - - - - low'd them, the earth
earth swal - - - - - - low'd them, the earth swal - - - -
- - - - - - - - - - - - - - low'd them, the earth swal -
the earth swal - - - - - - - low'd them, the . . earth swal-low'd,
the earth swal - low'd them, the earth swal - - - - - - - - low'd,
swal - low'd, swal - - - - - - low'd them, the earth swal - - - -
- - - - - - - - - - - - - - low'd them, the earth swal -
the earth swal - - - - - - - low'd them, the . . earth swal-low'd,
f

swal-low'd them, swal
low'd them, the earth swal
low'd them, swal
swal - low'd them, the . . earth . . swal
the earth . . . swal
low'd them, swal - low'd, swal - low'd,
low'd them, swallow'd, swal - low'd, swal - low'd,
swal - low'd them, the . . earth . . swal
low'd, swal - low'd them.
low'd them.
low'd them.
low'd them.
low'd them, the earth swal - low'd them.
swal - low'd, . . swal - low'd them.
swal - low'd, the . . earth swal - low'd them.
low'd them.

Duet.—"THOU IN THY MERCY."

Thou hast gui-ded them in Thy strength, un - - to Thy

strength . . un - - to Thy ho - ly ha-bi-

ho - ly ha-bi-ta - - - - -

- ta - - - - -

- - - tion.

- - - tion.

Thou hast gui-ded them

Thou hast gui-ded them in Thy strength,

in Thy strength, un - to Thy ho - ly ha - bi - ta-tion,

un - to Thy

Thou hast guided them in Thy strength,

ho - ly ha - bi - ta - tion, Thou hast gui-ded them in Thy strength,

un - to Thy ho - - - - - ly ha - bi - tion.

un - to Thy ho - - ly ha - bi - ta - tion.

DOUBLE CHORUS.—"THE PEOPLE SHALL HEAR."

1st TREBLE.

1st ALTO.

1st TENOR. (8ve. lower).

1st BASS.

2nd TREBLE.

2nd ALTO.

2nd TENOR. (8ve. lower).

2nd BASS.

PIANO. ♩=80.

The peo - ple shall

The peo - ple shall

till Thy people pass o-ver, O Lord, till Thy people pass o - ver,

till Thy people pass o-ver, O Lord, Thy peo-ple

till Thy people pass o-ver, O Lord,

till Thy people pass o - - ver,

till Thy people pass o-ver, O Lord, Thy peo-ple

till Thy people pass o-ver, O Lord, Thy peo-ple

till Thy people pass o-ver, O Lord,

till Thy people pass o - - ver,

mf

which Thou hast purcha-sed, till Thy people pass o - ver, O Lord,

which Thou hast pur-cha-sed, till Thy people pass o-ver, O

which Thou hast purcha - sed, till Thy people pass o - ver, O Lord,

which Thou hast pur-cha - sed, till Thy people pass o - ver, O Lord, they shall be as

which Thou hast pur-cha-sed, till Thy people pass o - ver, O Lord,

which Thou hast pur-cha-sed, till Thy people pass o-ver, O

which Thou hast pur-chased, till Thy people pass o - ver, O Lord,

which Thou hast pur-cha - sed, till Thy people pass o - ver, O Lord, they shall be as

f

AIR.—" THOU SHALT BRING THEM IN."

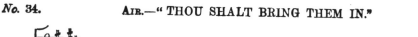

VOICE.

Largo e mezzo piano.

PIANO.
♩=96.

ALTO SOLO.

Thou shalt bring them in,   Thou shalt bring them in,   and

plant them in the moun - - - - - tain of Thine in - he - ritance,

in the place, . . . O Lord, which Thou hast made, ...

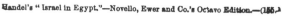

Handel's " Israel in Egypt."—Novello, Ewer and Co.'s Octavo Edition.—(155.)

which Thou hast made, for Thee to dwell in, for Thee to dwell in, to

dwell . . . . . . in,

in the sanc - tu - a - -

- - ry, O Lord, which Thy hands have e -

- sta - - - - - - - - - blish-ed,

in the sanc - - - tu -

- a - - - ry, which Thy

hands have e - sta - - - blish- ed, which Thy

Adagio.

hands have e- sta-blish-ed.

RECIT.—"FOR THE HORSE OF PHARAOH.

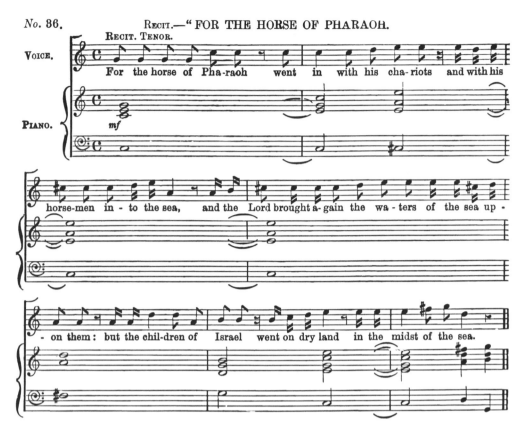

RECIT. TENOR.

VOICE.

PIANO.

mf

For the horse of Pha-raoh went in with his cha-riots and with his horse-men in - to the sea, and the Lord brought a-gain the wa-ters of the sea up - on them: but the chil-dren of Israel went on dry land in the midst of the sea.

DOUBLE CHORUS.—"THE LORD SHALL REIGN."

A tempo giusto.

1st TREBLE.

1st ALTO.

The Lord shall reign for e - ver and e - - -

1st TENOR (8ve. lower).

The Lord shall reign for e - ver and e - - -

1st BASS.

2nd TREBLE.

2nd ALTO.

The Lord shall reign for e - ver and e - - -

2nd TENOR (8ve. lower).

The Lord shall reign for e - ver and e - - -

2nd BASS.

A tempo giusto.

PIANO.

♩ = 88.

f

L

Handel's "Israel in Egypt."—Novello, Ewer and Co.'s Octavo Edition.

No. 38. RECIT.—"AND MIRIAM THE PROPHETESS."

VOICE.

RECIT. TENOR.

And Mi-ri-am the prophetess, the sis-ter of Aa-ron, took a tim-brel in her hand, and all the

PIANO.

mf

women went out af-ter her with timbrels and with dances, and Miriam an-swered them.

Handel's " Israel in Egypt."—Novello, Ewer and

and his rider, the horse and his rider hath He thrown in-to the sea, the
and his rider, the horse and his rider hath He thrown in-to the sea, the
and his rider, the horse and his rider hath He thrown in-to the sea, the
and his rider, the horse and his rider hath He thrown in-to the sea, the
rider, the horse and his rider hath He thrown, hath He thrown in-to the sea, the
rider, the horse and his rider hath He thrown, hath He thrown in-to the sea, the
rider, the horse and his rider hath He thrown, hath He thrown in-to the sea, the
rider, the horse and his rider hath He thrown, hath He thrown in-to the sea, the
horse and his ri-der, the horse and his ri-der, the horse and his rider, the horse and his rider hath
horse and his ri-der, the horse and his ri-der, the horse and his rider, the horse and his rider hath
horse and his ri-der, the horse and his ri-der, the horse and his rider, the horse and his rider hath
horse and his ri-der, the horse and his ri-der, the horse and his rider, the horse and his rider hath
horse and his ri-der, the horse and his ri-der, the horse and his rider, the horse and his rider hath
horse and his ri-der, the horse and his ri-der, the horse and his rider, the horse and his rider hath
horse and his ri-der, the horse and his ri-der, the horse and his rider, the horse and his rider hath
horse and his ri-der, the horse and his ri-der. the horse and his rider, the horse and his rider hath
ff

He thrown in-to the sea, the horse and his ri-der, the horse and his ri-der hath

He thrown in-to the sea, the horse and his ri-der, the horse and his ri der hath

He thrown in-to the sea, the horse and his ri-der, the horse and his ri-der hath

He thrown in-to the sea, the horse and his ri-der, the horse and his ri-der hath

He thrown in-to the sea, the horse and his ri-der, the horse and his ri-der hath

He thrown in-to the sea, the horse and his ri-der, the horse and his ri-der hath

He thrown in-to the sea, the horse and his ri-der, the horse and his ri-der hath

He thrown in-to the sea. I will

He thrown in-to the sea.

He thrown in-to the sea.

He thrown in-to the sea. I will sing . . . . .

He thrown in-to the sea. I will

He thrown in-to the sea.

He thrown in-to the sea.

He thrown in-to the sea. I will sing . . . . .

Printed and bound in Great Britain by
Caligraving Limited Thetford Norfolk

INDEX TO ISRAEL IN EGYPT.

NOVELLO'S EDITION.

PART THE FIRST.

PART THE SECOND.